WILLIAM MCKINLEY

A Life from Beginning to End

BY HOURLY HISTORY

Copyright © 2025 by Hourly History.

All rights reserved.

Table of Contents

Introduction
Called to Serve
In the Heat of Battle
Legal Career
Love, Marriage, and Politics
Tariffs, Tariffs, and More Tariffs!
The Road to the White House
The Cost of War
McKinley's Manifest Destiny
Assassination
Conclusion
Bibliography

Introduction

William McKinley was born on January 29, 1843, in the great state of Ohio. He hailed from a long line of ironmasters, blacksmiths, and manufacturers. On his father's side, he was descended from Scotch-Irish—often known as the "Ulster Scots"—who had emigrated to the New World from Northern Ireland in search of religious and economic freedom. These Presbyterians, with their strict Calvinism, became early industrialists in America. On his mother's side, his forebears were Dutch blacksmiths who established an iron furnace near Doylestown, Pennsylvania, where they produced cannonballs for the American Revolutionary War.

Both lines of McKinley's descendants were drawn to the iron ore deposits of the Mahoning Valley near Youngstown, where the so-called "kidney ore" laid the foundation of the local steel industry. The McKinleys established an iron business in New Lisbon, Ohio, and contributed to early furnace operations that produced rolled iron bars and other cast-iron products. William's father, William McKinley Sr., was born here in New Lisbon but later moved to Niles, Ohio, where he operated an iron furnace and rolling mill. It was in Niles that William Sr. met and married Nancy Allison. They would have nine children together, the seventh being William Jr.

When young William was about ten years old, his parents decided to pick up stakes and move on over to Poland, Ohio. It was here in Poland that William McKinley's formal education would begin in earnest. Because the senior McKinley was not well educated himself, he was determined to give his children a better education. For that reason, the family resettled in Poland, which had a better school. Young William proved to be a dedicated scholar who devoted considerable time to his studies. He also helped to organize his school's Debating and Literary Society, where he learned the art of oratory and debate.

William graduated from Poland Seminary School in 1859 when he was 16 years old. It was after finishing seminary school that McKinley enrolled at Allegheny College in Meadville, Pennsylvania. He did well there and was soon made an honorary member of the school's esteemed Sigma Alpha Epsilon fraternal order. But apparently not everything worked out quite so well at Allegheny, and after one year, William became burned out. When he returned home, he was both physically ill and mentally distressed. The exact cause of McKinley's feelings of unease is not entirely clear, but it was after he returned home from Allegheny that all hell broke loose on the national stage.

Shortly after President Abraham Lincoln was sworn into office in 1861, several Southern slave-holding states decided to secede from the Union. It was this rupture which led to the start of the American Civil War that April. At the outset of the war, young Ohioan men, just like William McKinley, were eager to do their part. And as the drums of war beat ever faster in the North, McKinley made his way down to the office of a state-run militia (called the Poland Guards) and made clear his intention to serve.

The nation had descended into terrible chaos, yet in the midst of this calamity, this young man suddenly felt some clarity of purpose. He had been a young man adrift, but now he knew exactly what needed to be done. No matter what the future might bring, he was determined to serve his country in any way he could.

Chapter One

Called to Serve

"If it be my lot to fall, I want to fall at my post and have it said that I fell in defense of my country in honor of the glorious stars and stripes."

—William McKinley

In June 1861, William McKinley became an official part of the 23rd Ohio Volunteer Infantry. He was barely 18 years old at the time. Always fairly short in stature, he stood at around 5 foot 7 (170 centimeters) and weighed about 125 pounds (57 kilograms). As such, this youngster cut a small figure in uniform. But if his fellow soldiers were tempted to not take him seriously due to either his youth or his small stature, William McKinley was quick to remind them that he was just as determined as anyone else to win the war.

The officer in charge of McKinley's unit was none other than the future president Rutherford B. Hayes. Hayes, who was a major in the army, was well-known in political circles and already a rising star in the Republican Party at the time. The first task that Major Hayes gave those under his charge was building their own barracks. Once they had a proper place to sleep, the troops were then relentlessly drilled on how to march, how to use their weapons, and how to guard their camp.

As patriotic as McKinley and his fellow soldiers might have been, there were many unforeseen challenges at the start of the war. No one really knew where it would all lead. In many ways, the federal government had been caught off guard and was still trying to play catch-up. Part of the problem was that Abraham Lincoln had just been sworn in when the states seceded. This caused quite a bit of chaos in what otherwise should have been a routine transfer of power.

In fact, things were so out of order that by the time the war erupted, there often weren't enough uniforms to go around. It's said that some members of McKinley's unit, rather than being able to don a crisp new uniform, were practically threadbare. What's more, bedding wasn't available for most of them. McKinley later recalled that during these early days of service, he slept on nothing more than a wooden board and had to use his own overcoat as a blanket just to keep warm. Such conditions were not exactly reassuring to the newfound recruits in the armed forces, to say the least.

Even the weapons were a problem. The first shipment of arms that McKinley's unit received was hopelessly antiquated. The old rifles they were given likely wouldn't have helped them much in combat. But fortunately for McKinley and company, as soon as Lincoln was able to get his house in order in Washington, DC, and the factories of the North started humming with the full backing of the federal government, all of these things would change.

Chapter Two

In the Heat of Battle

"They taught me a great deal. I was but a schoolboy when I went into the army, and that first year was a formative period in my life, during which I learned much of men and facts."

—William McKinley

On September 10, 1861, William McKinley engaged in combat for the first time. The battle began at the site of Carnifex Ferry in West Virginia. It was certainly quite an awakening to the horrors of war. Many young men might start out as patriotic idealists, in love with the notion of serving their country, but once the bullets start to fly and the devastating toll of death and destruction is made clear, much of that romanticism tends to go by the wayside.

William McKinley and his young compatriots were likely shocked to see all the blood and gore as men were torn to pieces by artillery fire. Although McKinley kept a brave face throughout, it was noted that he requested counseling with the military chaplain after this first round of fighting concluded. This is perhaps an indication that the young McKinley already had some things he wished to get off his chest in regard to what he had experienced.

Fortunately for William McKinley, he wouldn't have to be on the front lines of the war much longer. His superior officers apparently saw something valuable in the bright, pleasant young man and decided to make him a clerk. This meant that he would be working directly with the quartermaster, handling the everyday affairs of supplying the troops and other matters of consequence. Another reason why McKinley was likely picked for this position was the fact that he had a higher education level than most of his peers. While it's true that he didn't finish his commitments at Allegheny, he at least had some higher-level schooling under his belt, whereas many of his fellow soldiers likely didn't even have as much as an eighth-grade education.

At any rate, William McKinley apparently did a good job with the tasks he was given, and on April 15, 1862, he was promoted to the post of commissary sergeant. This was another supply-side role, which had him responsible for allocating food for the troops as well as the animals they kept with them. Horses, of course, were in frequent use by the army, and if they didn't have enough food, they wouldn't be able to serve their purpose. Obtaining proper horse feed, therefore, was absolutely crucial to the war effort. McKinley and his unit certainly needed fast (and well-fed) horses, for they were constantly on the move.

It's said that during the summer of 1862, they were constantly circling around Maryland, which had become a hotbed of Confederate troop movement. If the Confederates wished to invade the Northeast, Maryland would likely be the corridor through which they would have marched. Things then came to a head on September 14, 1862, when McKinley and his troops engaged in battle with Confederate forces in the vicinity of South Mountain. McKinley's unit was able to rally and quickly gained the upper hand as they pushed the Confederates back. The fighting took its toll, however, and Rutherford B. Hayes himself was injured in the melee.

More was to come, for just a few days later, the troops reconvened and met along a stream near Sharpsburg called Antietam. It was here, of course, that the infamous Battle of Antietam would be fought. Once again, the Union forces were victorious and forced the Confederate troops south all the way back to Virginia, but nevertheless, it was a terrible battle in terms of lives lost. Some 24,000 had been killed or wounded.

Here, McKinley played a pivotal role, risking life and limb to ferry supplies back and forth to Union forces. It might not seem like a big deal—but it was. McKinley was daring in his forays across that terrible battlefield, and he was very lucky not to have taken a bullet for his efforts. He was rewarded for his heroism and promoted to an officer; by March 1863, he had reached the rank of first lieutenant.

In the aftermath of the Battle of Antietam, the 23rd wintered in West Virginia. Hayes was still recovering from his injuries at this point, and his wife Lucy came to camp to aid in his healing process. It's said that McKinley got to know both of them quite well and that the older couple almost became like a second set of parents to him. At this point, Rutherford B. Hayes—who obviously valued McKinley's loyalty—made him his aide-de-camp as well as an acting assistant quartermaster.

After Hayes had sufficiently recovered, the 23rd received new marching orders from General George Crook. They were told to head into the Confederate stronghold of Virginia and do what they could to sabotage Confederate railways there. Destroying the rail lines used by the Confederates was of strategic importance since it would not only interrupt travel but—more importantly—the flow of supplies to the Confederacy.

On May 9, 1864, while in the midst of this effort, they once again engaged Confederate forces in combat. The 23rd ultimately prevailed, but their victory was once again a terribly costly affair. After this terrible battle had run its course, the 23rd made its way back to Meadow Bluff, West Virginia. It was a rough march over several miles of challenging terrain. Many of the soldiers' shoes were so worn they could hardly even be called shoes anymore. Nevertheless, they made it back to higher ground, though they didn't have long to rest before they were once again in the thick of things.

In July, the 23rd Ohio Volunteer Infantry, as part of Crook's army, faced off against an aggressive group of Confederates under the leadership of one Jubal Anderson Early. Early was a career soldier and had been quite experienced in the art of warfare even before the Civil War had broken out. He had attended West Point alongside several of his Union peers and had even served alongside them during the Mexican-American War. By the outbreak of the

Civil War, however, this Southerner sided with the Confederacy that had taken hold of the South. He quickly gained recognition as a capable commander.

The forces led by Early struck William McKinley's unit on July 24, 1864, inflicting terrible casualties. McKinley was serving as a special assistant for Major Hayes at the time and was caught right in the middle of this buzzsaw of bullets. Hayes needed to communicate with another unit under his oversight—the 13th West Virginia Infantry—but found himself completely caught off guard. He knew that the 13th would soon be annihilated if they didn't take action. He needed them to retreat, but without his order, they wouldn't do so.

It was the daring McKinley who didn't hesitate to ride through the thick of the bullets to personally deliver the message. He rode like mad across an active battlefield, dodging bullets all along the way. He reached the 13th, informed them of Rutherford's order to pull back, and then rode right back through enemy fire to get back to the 23rd. After he returned unscathed, he accompanied the 23rd Ohio Volunteer Infantry's own retreat through the wilderness. Owing to this latest round of heroism, William McKinley was made a captain.

McKinley continued to serve with distinction throughout the remainder of the war, and just as the war was coming to a close, he received another honor; on March 13, 1865, he was made a brevet major. The Confederacy was finally defeated in the meantime when General Robert E. Lee surrendered in April 1865. The war was over, and now William McKinley had to figure out what to do with the rest of his life.

Chapter Three

Legal Career

"Let us ever remember that our interest is in concord, not in conflict; and that our real eminence rests in victories of peace, not those of war."

—William McKinley

William McKinley was such a good soldier that he likely could have continued rising through the ranks in the army even after the war had ended, but it was his own father who ultimately dissuaded him. William Sr. reportedly advised his son that there was no future for soldiers during peacetime, and McKinley apparently took his father at his word.

 The younger McKinley ultimately decided to leave the army and head back to the Ohio family home so that he could study law. Studying law back then, of course, had a whole different meaning than it does today. In many cases, it quite literally entailed someone hunkering down in a room somewhere and studying legal textbooks.

There was often no need for any sort of college degree; all one had to do was study the law and then take a test to get certified. If they passed, that was it; they were an attorney.

Back in William McKinley's day, it was common practice to combine what was essentially a hands-on internship with studying. This often meant holing up in the office of an already practicing attorney. Here, one could both watch and perhaps even participate in the rigors of law, even while poring over legal texts. McKinley was able to secure just such an arrangement with a local lawyer by the name of Charles Glidden. McKinley became his understudy, watching everything he did while he studiously pored over legal texts in his free time. Even though this would have been enough back in those days, Glidden apparently insisted that McKinley would be better served if he actually went to an official law school.

While one could still study law independently at that time, law schools were just starting to become more common in the late 1860s. As such, with a little financial help from his parents, legal understudy William McKinley went off to enroll at the Albany Law School in Albany, New York. Unlike his aborted stint at Allegheny, McKinley apparently loved the experience. Battle-hardened and fresh from the horrors of the Civil War, he was most certainly much more mature this time around, and that likely had a lot to do with it. Instead of becoming homesick and distressed, this tough soldier apparently had the time of his life. He was quite sociable in Albany and went to all the latest parties and get-togethers. He also made it a habit to haunt the local theater. McKinley was also keenly interested in the political scene, and Albany, being the capital of New York state, proved to be a hub of constantly ongoing political activity.

After he finished his coursework in Albany, McKinley headed straight back to Ohio, where he passed the state bar exam without any problem. He was then officially made a licensed attorney in March 1867 when he was 24 years old. In his efforts to set up his own practice, he decided to set up shop in Canton, Ohio. The town was growing and was not too far from his old stomping grounds of Poland. His office was small and modest, but McKinley was sure to make quick connections that brought him attention as an up-and-coming young lawyer.

Among other things, he befriended a prominent local attorney by the name of George W. Belden, who happened to have his own office nearby. McKinley's moment of truth came when

Belden suddenly took ill and asked for McKinley to fill in for him. The matter was apparently time-sensitive, and McKinley would be needed to stand in for a legal case which was set to take place the following day. Though he was nervous about the prospect, he knew it was now or never and decided to give it a shot. The night before, full of both anticipation and anxiety, William McKinley essentially pulled an all-nighter, cramming for the case. His efforts apparently paid off because he ended up winning it.

Thanks to the talent and determination that McKinley displayed, Belden decided to take him on as a partner in his law firm. From this point on, McKinley began to earn a reputation as a great legal and political mind. As such, he became quite influential in the local political scene. His connections to Rutherford B. Hayes would then come to prominence when the old army major ran for the governor of Ohio on the Republican ticket. McKinley vigorously stumped for his old commander and gave frequent talks about the man's virtues both on and off the battlefield. Hayes ultimately won the election and became Ohio's next governor.

On the national stage, in the meantime, former Union General Ulysses S. Grant had decided to run for president as the Republican candidate.

McKinley was likewise enthusiastic about Grant's prospects and once again hit the campaign trail. He even went so far as to put up so-called "Grant Clubs," which were essentially fan clubs that did everything they could to enhance Grant's name recognition with the public. The old war hero ultimately triumphed and became the 18th president of the United States.

William McKinley was now an experienced and known political operator on both the local and the national stage. It wasn't long before it was suggested that he himself should run for office. McKinley finally made good on this inclination in 1869 when he ran as county prosecutor for the Republicans. Even though he faced fierce opposition from the Democrats, McKinley beat back his opponents. This was just the first of many political triumphs that William McKinley would have in store.

Chapter Four

Love, Marriage, and Politics

"Before I went to Congress, I had $10,000 and a practice worth $10,000 a year. Now I haven't either."

—William McKinley

It was in 1870 that the newly elected William McKinley finally began to think of something other than work and politics. That fateful year, he embarked upon the courtship of a certain Ida Saxton. Saxton hailed from a rather affluent family of bankers in Canton, Ohio, and actually worked at her father's bank when she first met McKinley. She had attended private school, traveled the world, and hailed from what was considered the upper strata of society at the time. McKinley figured she was a good match and pursued her with the same vigor that he pursued with just about everything else.

Matters apparently came to a head one fine evening when they stood under the romantic glare of the moon, and William asked Ida to marry him. She didn't hesitate to say yes, and the couple were duly wed on January 25, 1871. The crowd who gathered at the Presbyterian church where the ceremony was held included several notables, including the then-governor of Ohio, Rutherford B. Hayes. It was apparently a happy occasion, and the honeymoon was even happier. Their union would ultimately produce two children: Katherine, born on Christmas Day 1871, and Ida, born in 1873.

Not all good things last forever, however, and the couple was soon beset with a whole string of tragedies. Shortly after giving birth to Katherine, Ida's own mother abruptly perished. Ida was absolutely heartbroken at the loss. She was still in the midst of this grief when her second daughter and namesake Ida was born. Shortly after little baby Ida's birth, she too perished. The back-to-back losses of her mother and then her second child seemed to take a heavy toll on Ida McKinley. She had been perfectly happy and healthy before, but suddenly she was depressed and beset with all manner of health problems. She deteriorated so badly that she was virtually bedridden.

The situation would become even worse in 1875 when the couple's only surviving daughter Katherine died from a bad case of typhoid fever when she was just three years old. Ida was now absolutely inconsolable and even spoke openly of her fears that her husband William might be the next to go. It's not a pleasant thought for anyone to dwell on mortality—much less to have one's spouse constantly prophesy about one's impending demise. Nevertheless, William McKinley stood by his wife's side and was determined to see her through the darkness that had overtaken her life.

It was perhaps as a means to better deal with that said darkness that William McKinley threw himself headlong into politics. He decided in 1876 that he would run for Congress for Ohio's eastern district. Even as he set his sights on higher office, that very election year his old friend and mentor, Rutherford B. Hayes, set his sights on the presidency. Once again, McKinley became a cheerleader for Hayes, doing everything he could to get the Ohio governor promoted to the office of president. These efforts paid off, and Rutherford B. Hayes, riding high on a surging tide of enthusiasm for Republicans, became the 19th president of the United States with a strong Republican majority in the House of

Representatives. This strong majority included the newly elected Congressman William McKinley.

That meant both William and Ida would have a new address for the time being, so they packed their bags and headed for Washington, DC. It was likely a good change for Ida, as the new scenery helped take her mind off the tragedies that had taken place in her native Ohio. The heady world of DC politics would serve as a welcome distraction for them both.

Chapter Five

Tariffs, Tariffs, and More Tariffs!

"I do not prize the word cheap. It is not a word of inspiration. It is the badge of poverty. The signal of distress. Cheap merchandise means cheap men and cheap men—a cheap country."

—William McKinley

Once newly elected Congressman William McKinley had arrived in Washington, DC, Ida took on the traditional role of hostess. However, her frequent bouts of sickness usually rendered her unable to help much. She did receive some visitors but was often unwell during these functions and was frequently seen propped up with a pillow as if she could hardly move. She rarely attended functions with her husband, making William McKinley appear almost as if he were a bachelor.

Nevertheless, McKinley was a strong and spirited man, and he was able to hold his own with the best of them—even without his wife by his side. He proved to be a popular figure in politics, and he was easily re-elected in 1878 and again in 1880. However, during the 1882 term, the Democrats were up to some political chicanery and had redrawn districts to make them more friendly to Democratic candidates. This made the 1882 election much more difficult. McKinley initially eked out a narrow victory over his opponent Jonathan Wallace, winning by just eight votes. But when Wallace cried foul and challenged the election results, the House Committee on Elections took a second look and ultimately decided that Wallace was the winner, forcing McKinley out of office.

This loss meant William had to pack his things, leave Washington, DC, and return back to Canton. He could have given up on politics and gone back to practicing law, but something about the narrow defeat stuck with him and made him want to continue the fight. He ran once again in 1884, and this time around, he prevailed. McKinley was placed on the Ways and Means Committee, where he was able to take a long, hard look at the nation's fiscal policies. It was here that he developed a love affair with the concept of tariffs.

In international commerce, a tariff is essentially a tax placed upon goods imported into the country. McKinley saw tariffs as both a tool to leverage negotiations with other nations as well as a source of revenue for the nation as a whole. One could think of it as a form of external revenue rather than internal revenue since rather than taxing American citizens, it placed a tax on other nations who wanted to do business with America. Tariffs were also a means to convince local manufacturers to keep products within the United States so they wouldn't have to rely on imports that are subject to high tariffs. The world has changed considerably since then, and arguments about the effectiveness of tariffs are currently a matter of great debate. But back in McKinley's day, tariffs were often seen as a reliable means of keeping manufacturing in the United States, thereby ensuring that the American worker had a decent nine-to-five job.

For his part, William McKinley loved tariffs, and he was perhaps the perfect person to promote them. He understood tariffs and their impact, and he was adept at explaining these ideas in terms the average American (whether they liked tariffs or not) could understand—all of which was crucial in getting others to see the value (at least from McKinley's perspective) in his strategy of implementing high tariffs on foreign goods. McKinley would make full use of tariffs when he was later elected to the presidency. Until then, however, the political landscape was in for a complete shake-up when a Democrat by the name of Grover Cleveland was elected president in 1884.

Cleveland was no fan of tariffs. He ran as a reformer, and to him tariffs were just another example of the government overreach he sought to reform. He appealed to farmers, in particular, who seemed to have the most to lose by high tariffs. President Cleveland's first term was a mixed bag, however, and he was ultimately defeated by Indiana attorney-turned-Republican standard bearer Benjamin Harrison in 1888. Prior to Benjamin Harrison receiving his party's nomination, there was chatter that William McKinley might make a good long-shot candidate, though the nomination ultimately fell on Harrison.

Since Grover Cleveland had presented himself as being against tariffs, the Republicans took issue with his stance during the 1888 campaign. They essentially presented Cleveland as being against the protection of American trade since tariffs were viewed as protective measures to ensure fair trade. Upon Benjamin Harrison's rise to the presidency, as is often the case in politics, he took his election as a rebuke of Grover Cleveland's policies and went full steam in the opposite direction. As such, he embraced tariffs and, in particular, William McKinley's vision of them. He even went so far as to name his new legislation the McKinley Tariff Bill.

This complex raft of tariffs was signed by President Harrison and made into law on November 1, 1890. The tariffs weren't all they were cracked up to be, however, and caused a sudden rise in prices foisted onto the backs of consumers. These price hikes led to a political backlash against the Republicans, and Congressman McKinley was not re-elected in 1890. The ever-changing winds of political fate ultimately helped Grover Cleveland make a historic comeback. He defeated Harrison in the presidential election and, in 1892, became the first president to be elected to a non-consecutive term.

Chapter Six

The Road to the White House

"That's all a man can hope for during his lifetime—to set an example—and when he is dead, to be an inspiration for history."

—William McKinley

Even though he was voted out of Congress, William McKinley couldn't leave politics behind. Instead, he simply switched gears and ran for governor of Ohio in 1891. He won this contest and set about refashioning his home state in his own image. His efforts worked for Ohio, and he proved to be a popular governor who was re-elected for a second term in 1893.

Perhaps realizing how much the little guy felt slighted in the previous experimentation with tariffs, McKinley made himself an advocate for factory workers during his time as governor. He championed labor unions and put forth measures to make Ohio factories safer for workers. But even

William McKinley had his limits, and when a labor strike threatened to get out of control, he didn't hesitate to use his authority as governor to break it up. Nevertheless, he remained quite popular as governor.

William McKinley proved to be so popular, in fact, that he was ultimately nominated to be the standard bearer for the Republicans in the 1896 presidential election. He had considerable support in this direction by way of influential businessman and industrialist Mark Hanna, who was at that time the chairman of the Republican National Committee. McKinley and Hanna were good friends and would remain close for the rest of McKinley's life. Meanwhile, the political winds of fate had shifted once again, and the public was now looking upon the Republicans much more favorably.

As much as Grover Cleveland had successfully attacked the Republicans over the cost of tariffs, his second term ended in an economic disaster that plunged the country into a recession. Since term limits had not yet been set in the United States, Cleveland could have possibly attempted a third term, but by the end of his second term, he was too unpopular even to consider such a thing. As such, the nomination for his party went to a young rising star of the Democrats—William Jennings Bryan.

For his part, Bryan embarked upon a whistle-stop-styled campaign in which he crisscrossed the country to meet large crowds as he stumped for policy positions he hoped would earn him a seat in the White House. McKinley, on the other hand, barely even left his house. He took the exact opposite approach by embarking upon what was dubbed the Front Porch Campaign. Rather than go out and speak to large crowds, McKinley held lavish spectacles right from his front porch in Canton, Ohio. Folks came from all around to hear the words of the presidential candidate. For whatever reason, McKinley's folksy front porch tactics seemed to work. Thousands of people would come to visit him on any given day, and he slowly but steadily built up his support without even breaking a sweat.

McKinley's campaign staff were also very efficient at getting out campaign materials, flooding the nation with posters, buttons, and booklets. Also aiding McKinley was his old friend Mark Hanna, who raised some 3.5 million dollars in campaign contributions, which was quite a hefty war chest of campaign funds back in those days. All this led to a decisive victory for William McKinley on election day. He managed to secure

271 electoral votes while his opponent obtained only 176. McKinley also won the popular vote by a considerable margin.

After he was sworn into office as the 25th US president on March 4, 1897, William McKinley hit the ground running. From the beginning, he sought to bring greater transparency to the office, and as part of that, he allowed the press to come and go as they pleased. It was in this newly transparent atmosphere that McKinley sought to restore much of the previous legislation on tariffs that Grover Cleveland had undone. He still believed that higher tariffs could bring in revenue and help ease the nation out of the economic downturn that had occurred during the previous administration. Still, President McKinley viewed tariffs more as a tool rather than an end goal in itself, and he was sure to leave enough wiggle room to allow himself to renegotiate trade with other nations on the fly, as he and any international trade partners saw fit.

Tariffs were still questionable in the eyes of many, but over the next couple of years, the economy began to make a rapid recovery. The debate is still out on how much the tariffs had to do with that recovery, but the McKinley administration was sure to take credit for it all the same. Yet financial matters would soon take a backseat when issues on the international stage came to the surface. In particular, the status of Cuba had become a point of contention. Cuba had been under Spanish control for centuries, but during McKinley's administration, vicious fighting erupted as Cuban revolutionaries attempted to throw off their colonial overlords in a bitter war of independence.

President McKinley, for his part, was initially determined to keep the United States out of this conflict. He figured it was up to the Cubans to work out their destiny on their own without any outside interference. But after Spain initiated a brutal crackdown on Cuba, America was forced to take notice of what was happening down in the Caribbean, just 90 miles (140 kilometers) south of Florida. The popular image of the Cuban revolutionary carrying on a struggle that supposedly echoed the United States' own war of independence against Britain took a strong hold of the American psyche. As such, there were increasingly vocal calls from many in the American public to take a more proactive stance to help the Cubans.

As altruistic as all of this might sound, one can't forget that there were definitely ulterior motives at play as well. Some wealthy investors in the United States, who had stakes in Cuba's thriving sugar plantations, wished to safeguard their own interests by ousting Spain from Cuba. Nevertheless, McKinley didn't like the idea of going to war with a European power and initially did everything he could to resist the call to combat. He sincerely hoped that cooler heads might prevail. Yet all that thinking would go right out the window on February 15, 1898.

That fateful day, an American ship, the USS *Maine*, suffered a catastrophic explosion and was quite literally blown right out of the water. To this day, no one is exactly sure what caused the explosion, but 266 sailors went to their deaths as a result. Even though Spain denied any hand in the incident, the public had already declared Spain's guilt, and now war was all but a foregone conclusion.

Chapter Seven

The Cost of War

"Too soon we forget. After a certain length of time, war takes on a romantic image and suggests excitement and adventure. Can we not remember that war is death and destruction? It is a hollow victory that is won at the expense of lost men and broken families."

—William McKinley

In the aftermath of the sinking of the USS *Maine*, President McKinley was forced to move America to a war footing—not so much by Spain but by an American public increasingly itching for war. Due to this popular pressure, McKinley requested some 50 million dollars from Congress in March 1898 to bolster the country's national defense. He used these funds to give a boost to the country's naval forces.

April 1898 then saw renewed skirmishes erupt between Cuban revolutionaries and Spanish forces. Citing the need to stabilize Cuba, McKinley asked Congress to give him the power to utilize the armed forces to safeguard this vested interest. No declaration of war was yet made, but the groundwork was clearly being laid out at this point—so much so that Spain beat the Americans to the punch by pre-emptively declaring war on the United States on April 24. The following day, the US officially reciprocated with its own declaration through the United States Congress.

President McKinley took his role as commander in chief of the armed forces very seriously. He had a war room established, which held multiple telegraph and telephone lines so that he could stay abreast of the conflict. This was very important since this war would not only be waged in and around Cuba but also in East Asia near what was then the Spanish possession of the Philippines.

By way of his communication lines in the war room, President McKinley ordered Commodore George Dewey, who was stationed in the Far East, to commence with a planned attack on the Spanish fleet, known as the Philippine Plan. On May 1, Dewey was able to corner the Spanish fleet parked in the Philippines and destroy it, delivering a major blow to the Spanish war effort early on. By contrast, the mobilization of the US Army proved to be a much slower process. It would be another month before troops were suitably mobilized and American boots were put on the ground in Cuba.

The first US troops arrived on Cuban soil on June 22, landing some 14 miles (22 kilometers) east of Santiago de Cuba. There was one unit among these land forces which would gain significant notoriety. It was led by General Leonard Wood as well as a certain colonel named Theodore Roosevelt. Prior to his volunteering to lead this outfit (which had subsequently been dubbed the Rough Riders), Roosevelt had been serving as the assistant secretary of the Navy. He was apparently so overcome with patriotism and a desire to get involved in as hands-on a way as possible that he immediately resigned from his post in the Navy and joined the Rough Riders at the outbreak of the war.

With Theodore Roosevelt leading the charge, this rough-and-tumble bunch reached the city of Santiago de Cuba on July 1, 1898. Soon, they were being fired upon by Spanish troops perched up in the San Juan Hills. Even though the Spanish had the high ground, Roosevelt knew there was no turning back, so he decided to charge head-on into the fray. He led his men on a successful charge up the San Juan Hills, which allowed them to overcome and overtake the Spanish positions. The Spanish soldiers who survived the onslaught were forced to make a hasty retreat, and by the end of the day, the US had managed to secure the Spanish fort in Santiago de Cuba.

The next blow for Spain came when what remained of their fleet was destroyed by the US Navy in Cuba. Right on the heels of this triumph, US troops landed in Puerto Rico. It seemed that nothing could stop the Americans, and soon Spain was actively suing for peace. Final terms were subsequently reached, and Spain ended up relinquishing Cuba as well as Puerto Rico, Guam, and the Philippines. While the US had no intention of annexing Cuba and allowed Cuban independence to play out, it did seize direct control of Puerto Rico, Guam, and the Philippines.

The taking of the Philippines was controversial in itself. President McKinley would later claim that it was his view that the Philippines was in such a chaotic state that just cutting it off and leaving it to drift would have been a recipe for disaster. Eventually, the Philippines would be granted its own independence after the Second World War, but Puerto Rico and Guam remain US territories to this very day. The status of these two US possessions remains a subject of hot debate. Statehood has occasionally been mentioned, but for now, both continue to be relegated to a state of territorial limbo.

The final terms of these agreements, meanwhile, were ratified by the United States Senate on February 6, 1899. The most immediate problem this would bring to the McKinley administration was the status of the Philippines. As mentioned, the Filipinos had been fighting to shake off the Spanish just like the Cubans, but unlike the Cubans, the US did not guarantee them an immediate path to independence. Filipino insurgents soon rose up to take on the American occupiers in what essentially became the next phase of their struggle.

It was in order to put down this insurgency that President McKinley sent 126,000 troops to the Philippines. This round of fighting only came to an end in 1901 when Filipino revolutionary Emilio Aguinaldo was taken into custody. After the dust had settled, an agreement was ultimately worked out with Emilio, and he promised to pledge allegiance to the American flag and persuaded his compatriots to do the same. After the fighting had subsided, the losses on both sides were quite staggering. It's said that thousands of US troops had been killed—a far greater number than had lost their lives during the Spanish-American War. The United States now had control of the Philippines and other extra-territorial possessions, but many began to wonder at what cost.

Chapter Eight

McKinley's Manifest Destiny

"We need Hawaii just as much and a good deal more than we did California. It is manifest destiny."

—William McKinley

Due to the sweeping territorial acquisitions that occurred under his administration, William McKinley would long be accused of imperialism. He certainly didn't set out to become an imperialist during his heyday of riding high on tariffs, but fate seemed to constantly conspire to put McKinley in prime position for imperialist ambition, whether he liked it or not. McKinley, after all, had resisted the war with Spain and the subsequent territorial gains it would bring about, but the war went forward regardless. He also initially resisted calls to annex the Pacific island of Hawaii.

Trouble had been brewing in Hawaii for some time, but initially such things didn't rank too high on McKinley's agenda. In 1893, a group of powerful sugar plantation owners staged a coup and overthrew the long-held Hawaiian monarchy, removing the Hawaiian Queen Liliuokalani from power. These oligarchs had petitioned then-President Benjamin Harrison to make Hawaii part of the United States, but the subsequent bill presented to Congress was rejected. Grover Cleveland then became president, and he rejected any such notion outright. Not to be deterred, the plantation owners who overthrew the queen had set up their own civilian government and elected their own president, a plantation owner by the name of Sanford Dole.

During the height of the Spanish-American War, McKinley looked into the matter and ultimately came out in favor of annexation. The US was already utilizing Hawaii's Pearl Harbor in operations against Spain, and McKinley could sense the strategic importance of long-term control of Hawaii. Many in Congress were also wary of Japanese expansion in the Pacific and figured if they didn't secure and safeguard the territory, the Japanese might take it for themselves. Ultimately, by way of a joint resolution through Congress, Hawaii was made a US territory on July 7, 1898.

It was riding high on all of these perceived wins and territorial acquisitions that President McKinley seemed all but certain to be re-elected as the 1900 presidential election neared. Along with the territorial conquests that excited the American electorate, the economy was on the rebound and humming along on all cylinders. As the presidential election came closer into view, McKinley had to make one important—and ultimately very fateful—decision. His previous running mate, Garret Hobart, had perished in 1899. He needed to make a new vice president pick—and he needed to make one quick. It didn't take him very long to consider the former assistant secretary of the Navy, Teddy Roosevelt.

Roosevelt became a hero during the Spanish-American War when he led the Rough Riders and had since been elected governor of his home state of New York. McKinley couldn't resist picking the popular Roosevelt in order to bolster his own support. The ticket that McKinley and Roosevelt put together proved to be unbeatable. Their opponent was the previously defeated William Jennings Bryan, who was ultimately trounced once again. McKinley repeated his same Front Porch Campaign style, and it paid off. He was re-elected in an electoral landslide.

William McKinley felt that he was given a mandate by the American people; he cited their votes cast for him as being their stamp of approval, and he promised to do even more for the nation during his second term. Little did he know how short his second term would ultimately be.

Chapter Nine

Assassination

"I killed President McKinley because I done my duty. I didn't believe one man should have so much service and another man should have none."

—Leon Czolgosz

During the first few weeks of his second term, President William McKinley outlined some pretty ambitious plans. Among them was a plan to cut a canal through the thin strip of land that connected North America to South America. He argued that it was crucial to create this shortcut so that shipping could easily cross from the Atlantic to the Pacific Ocean. Without the canal in place, shipping had to go on a long, arduous trip around the tip of South America in order to get from one coast to the other. The canal promised to cut this journey short by thousands of miles. Not only would it streamline commercial shipping, but as President McKinley argued, it would be of immense strategic worth to the US Navy since it would make it much easier to send warships from one coast of the United States to the other.

Although President McKinley wouldn't live to see its completion, it was under his administration that much of the groundwork for the Panama Canal was put in place. Early in 1900, in the meantime, a major international ruckus erupted with the so-called Boxer Rebellion in China. This rebellion was brought on by a group of Chinese martial artists who were fed up with what they viewed as foreign interference with their country. In previous decades, China had been forced to make many concessions in trade and other areas to outside powers, and these so-called "Boxers" were quite sick of it. And they weren't afraid to use violence to prove their point.

The Boxers apparently began attacking foreigners—including Americans—entirely at random. This led to the creation of an international force being dispatched to China, which included some 5,000 US soldiers. President McKinley made sure to safeguard Americans who were being threatened by this sudden outburst of xenophobic rage. He made sure that both American interests and the American people were protected while they operated out of China. McKinley's unilateral decision to dispatch troops without consulting the legislature set a precedent that led most of his successors to exert similar independent control over the military.

In Cuba, in the meantime, Cuban independence was proving to be not as straightforward as was first thought. The Cubans had presented their constitution to the US government for approval, only to be hit with an amendment known as the Platt Amendment. Championed by Republican Senator Orville Platt, the amendment made clear that should any political turbulence break out in Cuba, the United States had the right to send in the troops. Ironically, as a result of this very amendment, political turmoil did indeed erupt when the constitution passed on March 1, 1901. Despite massive protests in Havana, the US dug in its heels and refused to recognize Cuban independence until another constitutional convention was held and the amendment was enshrined within the constitution. Ultimately, the Cubans gained only a limited form of independence, and resentment would continue to simmer over the status of Cuba for the next several decades.

Despite these incidents, there was still time for celebration. On September 5, 1901, William McKinley arrived at the Pan-American Exposition in Buffalo, New York, where he gave a speech to attendees. McKinley then appeared at a reception held at the so-called Temple of Music the following day. As was customary for presidents back in those days, he was out in the open the whole time, and anyone who wanted to do him harm easily could have. Unfortunately for William McKinley, there was indeed someone in the crowd who intended to do just that. His name was Leon Czolgosz.

Czolgosz was an anarchist from Detroit who believed that all governments should be overthrown. It was later learned that he was an adherent of another radical by the name of Emma Goldman. Goldman was a Russian immigrant who subscribed to various socialist and anarchist views. At heart, she was a deeply frustrated individual who blamed society for many of her professional and personal problems. Despite these hangups, she was apparently a gifted speaker and was quite good at stirring up intense emotions among those who heard her speeches. Leon Czolgosz was apparently a big fan of hers, and he later admitted that it was after he heard one of Goldman's lectures that he was first inspired to assassinate President McKinley. Once word got out that Goldman had so clearly inspired Czolgosz, she herself was arrested on charges of conspiracy. She was ultimately released, but suspicion continued to follow her.

At any rate, it was a little after four pm on September 6 that Leon Czolgosz made his way to the front of the crowd and faced William McKinley. President McKinley, as friendly as he was, saw the young man and reached out to shake his hand. It was as he was seeking the man's hand in a gesture of friendship that Czolgosz pulled out a gun and opened fire. The gun had been obscured by a handkerchief. The cloth might have obscured the weapon from sight, but that little piece of fabric did nothing to stop the bullets that rocketed out of the gun's barrel. Out of this barrage, President McKinley was hit two times. As he was being pummeled with bullets, McKinley lost his balance and fell back into the arms of his security guards, who grabbed hold of the injured president and sought to steady him. All eyes had turned to the commotion by this point, and soon a mob descended upon Czolgosz, making sure that he didn't get away.

Just when it seemed as if the crowd was on the verge of tearing Leon Czolgosz limb from limb, McKinley intervened. It was only the injured president's measured words heard over the commotion—urging restraint and imploring the mob not to harm his assailant—that stayed their hand. McKinley was then taken to the hospital to have his wounds looked after. At the time, no one was quite sure how severe his injuries were. The doctors discovered that the first bullet had been deflected by a button, but McKinley wasn't quite so lucky with the second bullet since it had torn through his stomach. Nevertheless, it was indeed initially hoped that the president would be able to make a rebound.

After he lingered on for six days, McKinley began to grow worse. He couldn't eat, and he was in terrible pain. His temperature went through the roof. Gangrene set in, and the surrounding tissue began to rot due to the limited medical interventions available at the time. Doctors attempted to drain the infection and manage the ensuing sepsis with the antiseptic methods of the era, but their efforts were ultimately in vain. As he grew weaker and weaker, McKinley began to accept his fate. He told those who stood at his bedside that his passing would be God's will and not to fight it.

William McKinley ultimately perished in the early morning hours of September 14, 1901. He was 58 years old. His passing was met with great sadness, and extensive memorial services were put together to honor his memory. First, a smaller-scale funeral was held in Buffalo, New

York, before his casket was taken by train to lay in state at the capital, in Washington, DC. It was during this phase of his memorial services that countless mourners streamed by his casket as they said goodbye to the man who had been their president.

With McKinley's passing, a whole new exciting era would begin because his vice president, the extremely popular and charismatic Teddy Roosevelt, would become president by default. President Roosevelt would indeed go on to become one of the most popular US presidents of all time. He was, after all, one of the few presidents deemed worthy to have his face carved into Mount Rushmore. At any rate, once Roosevelt took over the office of the presidency, it served to ensure that much of William McKinley's own legacy would remain intact.

Conclusion

William McKinley was a man inclined to serve. One could argue whether or not the service that he rendered lived up to the right kind of aspirations, but his desire to serve was clear nonetheless. This desire was on full display during the outbreak of the American Civil War when, as a young man, he dared to risk life and limb in the service of the Union Army. During the war, he put his own life in danger on countless occasions to relay supplies or messages across enemy lines. This same sort of selfless sacrifice also came into play when he ran for political office.

McKinley was never the kind of politician who would use political wedge issues just to drum up votes. He simply had things that he believed in, and he ran on those principles. He didn't have to create any wedge issues or any other political drama to collect the votes. One of his most enduring traits in the world of politics, in fact, was that when he was debating a political opponent, McKinley wasn't so much trying to make them look bad as he was pleading with them to come around to his point of view. William McKinley never really saw an outright enemy, only those that needed to be persuaded.

He himself was persuaded by the American public during the lead-up to the Spanish-American War. It was the popular and headstrong feelings of the American populace that led to America's involvement in the push for Cuban independence. This war led to the defeat of an old-world imperial power and also signified America's own rise to dominance on the world stage. McKinley presided over a great crossroads in American history as he oversaw the transition from the America of the 1800s to the America of the 1900s. Yes, even though he was only 5 foot 7 (170 centimeters) in height, William McKinley still stands taller than most.

Bibliography

Armstrong, William Howard (2000). *Major McKinley: William McKinley and the Civil War.*

Gunderson, M. Megan (2009). *William McKinley.*

Phillips, Kevin (2003). *William McKinley.*

Riehecky, Janet (2004). *William McKinley: America's 25th President.*

Rove, Karl (2015). *The Triumph of William McKinley: Why the Election of 1896 Still Matters.*

Skrabec, R. Quentin (2008). *William McKinley: Apostle of Protectionism.*

Printed in Great Britain
by Amazon